Let's Make a

Salt Crystal

by Katie Chanez

NORWOOD HOUSE PRESS

Norwood House Press

For information regarding Norwood House Press, please visit our website at:
www.norwoodhousepress.com or call 866-565-2900.

PHOTO CREDITS: Cover: © Red Line Editorial; © Bunphot/iStockphoto, 13; © Imfoto/Shutterstock Images, 4; © Irrin0215/
iStockphoto, 8; © Marilyn Nieves/iStockphoto, 7; © Red Line Editorial, 19, 21, 22, 23, 24, 25, 27, 28; © Ruben Ramos/iStockphoto,
11; © RyersonClark/iStockphoto, 17; © Studio_Dagdagaz/iStockphoto, 14

Hardcover ISBN: 978-1-68450-840-2
Paperback ISBN: 978-1-68404-622-5

LIBRARY OF CONGRESS CATALOGING-IN-PUBLICATION DATA

Names: Chanez, Katie, author.
Title: Let's make a salt crystal / by Katie Chanez.
Description: Chicago : Norwood House Press, 2021. | Series: Make your own: science experiment! | Includes index. | Audience:
    Grades 2-3.
Identifiers: LCCN 2020001368 (print) | LCCN 2020001369 (ebook) | ISBN 9781684508402 (hardcover) | ISBN 9781684046225
    (paperback) | ISBN 9781684046287 (pdf)
Subjects: LCSH: Salt crystals--Experiments--Juvenile literature. | Salt--Juvenile literature. | Science--Experiments--Juvenile literature.
Classification: LCC QD189 .C45 2020 (print) | LCC QD189 (ebook) | DDC 546/.34--dc23
LC record available at https://lccn.loc.gov/2020001368
LC ebook record available at https://lccn.loc.gov/2020001369

328N—072020
Manufactured in the United States of America in North Mankato, Minnesota.

Contents

Some crystals, such as sapphires, are very rare and valuable.

CHAPTER 1

All about Crystals

Crystals are solids. They are made of particles that are arranged in a pattern. Crystals are natural materials. They form from nonliving materials called **minerals**. Ice is a crystal. It forms naturally, is not alive, and is a solid. Liquid water forms naturally and is not alive, but it is not a solid. That means it is not a crystal.

Crystals surround us in everyday life. Gemstones such as diamonds and rubies are types of crystals. But crystals have other uses besides jewelry. People use crystals such as salt and sugar while cooking. A type of crystal called quartz can power a watch. The graphite in pencil lead is a type of crystal. Even snowflakes are crystals!

Everything in the universe is made of matter. This means minerals are made of matter. Matter is made of tiny pieces called **atoms**. Atoms can connect with other atoms to create a **molecule**. When this happens, a **chemical bond** forms. These bonds determine whether a mineral forms a crystal.

Writing causes the graphite crystal to break and stick to the paper.

Sometimes, atoms in a mineral connect in a regular order. This creates a pattern. The atoms continue to connect in this pattern. The atoms in one part of the crystal will be in the same order as atoms in another part. This pattern is what creates a crystal.

Not everything made of minerals is a crystal. Glass is made of minerals. But the atoms are not in a repeating pattern. Rocks are also made of minerals. Sometimes they even have pieces of crystal in them. But the rest of the rock is not a crystal. This is because the rest of the atoms are not in a pattern.

Crystals form when too many molecules are mixed into a gas or liquid. The atoms in solids cannot move around. But the atoms in liquids and gases can. When a gas or liquid is heated, its atoms move farther apart. This allows more molecules to be mixed in. The gas or liquid cools. Its atoms get closer together. Then there is not enough room for the extra molecules. This is called **supersaturation**.

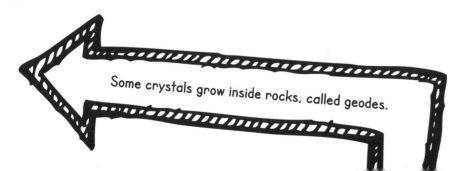

Some crystals grow inside rocks, called geodes.

The cooled gas or liquid cannot hold the extra molecules. The molecules must attach to a surface. Sometimes the molecules bump into each other. They connect. These actions create a **seed crystal**. More molecules attach to the seed crystal. This makes the crystal grow bigger and bigger. Crystals can grow to be several feet long! Large crystals need enough time, space, and materials to grow. Crystals can grow over hundreds or thousands of years.

Crystals come in several patterns. For example, some crystals' patterns are made of tiny cubes. Other patterns have sides of different lengths. The pattern of the atoms causes the shape of the crystals. Temperature, **pressure**, and the amount of space can

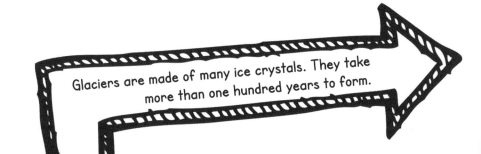

Glaciers are made of many ice crystals. They take more than one hundred years to form.

all affect a crystal's pattern and shape. These patterns can cause crystals to have very different properties. Even crystals that are made from the same mineral can have different patterns. Graphite and diamonds are crystals. They are both made from carbon. Graphite crystals are very thin sheets stacked together. This is a simple pattern. The thin sheets make graphite very soft. Pencil lead is made of graphite. When you use a pencil, pieces of graphite break and stick to the paper. In contrast, the atoms in diamonds connect in a very complicated pattern. This pattern makes diamonds the strongest material in nature.

Salt Crystal Molecule

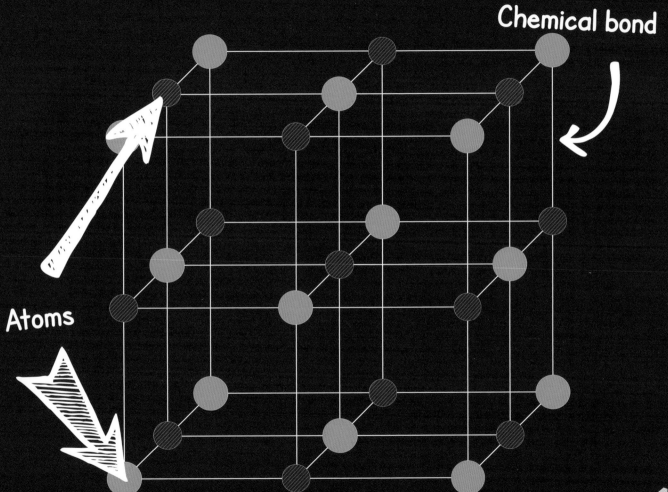

Chemical bond

Atoms

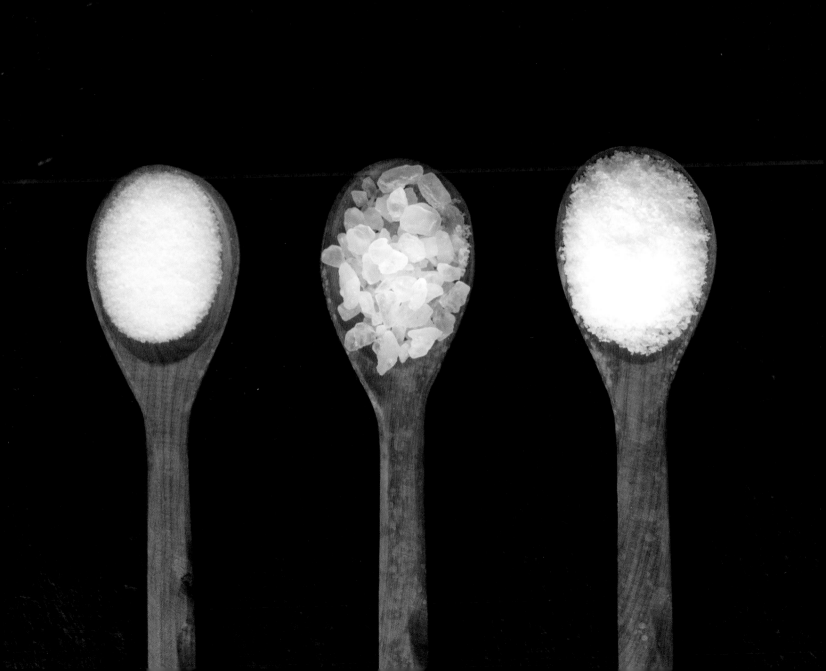

CHAPTER 2

Make Your Own Salt Crystal

Crystals can take hundreds or thousands of years to grow. But you can make a salt crystal in a few days! The tiny pieces of salt you put on your food are already crystals. If you look at salt with a microscope, the salt crystals look like tiny cubes.

Crystals form when a gas or liquid becomes supersaturated. For your experiment, you will use distilled water.

Regular water has minerals in it. Distilled water does not. This allows your salt to form a crystal without other minerals affecting it. Heating up the water causes the water molecules to move farther apart. There is room for more salt. When you mix salt in water, the salt **dissolves**. The salt molecules can go between the water molecules. But there is only a certain amount of room for the salt. The solution is **saturated** when the salt stops dissolving. As the water begins to cool, the molecules move closer together again. There is no longer enough room for all the salt. The mixture becomes supersaturated. The salt needs a new place to go.

The extra salt attaches to the sides and bottom of the container it is in. You will use a jar. But the jar is smooth. This makes it hard for

Boiling water can hold more salt than cold water can.

the salt to attach. String is not smooth. You can hang it in your jar. Salt crystals can attach to it more easily. Crystals will also form on any undissolved salt. But you want your crystal to grow on the string. The crystals that grow on the string are usually larger. You can remove any undissolved salt by pouring the water through a filter. Now your crystal will grow on the string.

The crystal stops growing when the mixture is no longer supersaturated. Over time, the salt molecules leave the water to form the crystal. The water **evaporates**. As the water evaporates, there is less water in the jar. But the salt molecules stay in the jar. Then there is still more salt in the water than there is room for. The water stays supersaturated. The salt continues to form crystals. This keeps happening until all the salt leaves the water.

This experiment uses hot water. You will need an adult to help. Glass can also break easily. It is important to be careful when moving your jar. You can keep growing your crystals for as long as you want. Some crystals will grow on the sides and bottom of the jar. If this happens, you can move the string with the crystals to a clean jar with more salt water. Your crystals will keep growing!

Materials Checklist

✓ Distilled water

✓ Table salt

✓ Spoon

✓ 1 cup measuring cup

✓ Glass jar

✓ Funnel

✓ Paper filter

✓ Scissors

✓ String

✓ Pencil or pen

✓ Microwave-safe dish

19

Be careful when removing the dish from the microwave. It will be hot!

CHAPTER 3

Science Experiment!

Now that you know how crystals form, put your knowledge to use and make your own!

1. Measure enough distilled water to fill your jar three-quarters of the way full. Pour the water into a microwave-safe container. Have an adult help you microwave the water until bubbles begin to form.

2. Add one cup of salt and stir until completely dissolved. Continue to add more salt a little bit at a time. Stir the salt until it dissolves. Do this every time you add salt. Stop adding salt when it stops dissolving no matter how much you stir.

3. Place the filter in the funnel. Place the funnel on top of the jar. Work with your adult helper and slowly pour the water through the funnel into the jar.

4. Cut a piece of string that is almost as long as the jar. Tie one end of the string to the middle of the pencil or pen.

5. Place the pencil on top of the jar so that the string is hanging in the water. Make sure the string does not touch the bottom or sides of the jar.

6. Wait until the jar is cool enough to touch.

7. Carefully place your jar in a cool, dark place. Choose somewhere where no one will bother it. Place a paper filter on top. This will keep dust off your jar.

8. Check on your jar every day. It can take several days for the crystals to grow. The longer you leave the jar, the bigger the crystals will get! When the crystals are the size you want, carefully lift the string out of the jar.

Make It Better!

Congratulations! You have grown salt crystals. Now see if there are ways to improve them. Use any of these changes and see how they affect your crystals.

- You used regular table salt to grow your crystals. However, there are many different salts, including sea salt and rock salt. How does changing the type of salt affect the growth of your crystals?

- Salts are not the only material that will form crystals. Rock candy is made of sugar crystals. Borax, a cleaning product with the mineral boron, also forms crystals. How is your crystal different when you try one of these materials?

Can you think of any ways that you could improve or change your crystals to make them better?

Glossary

atoms **(AT-uhmz):** Tiny things that are building blocks of all matter.

chemical bond **(KEM-uh-kuhl BOND):** A force that connects atoms or molecules together.

dissolves **(di-ZOLVZ):** Breaks apart and seems to disappear when mixed with a liquid.

evaporates **(i-VAP-uh-ratess):** Turns into a gas.

minerals **(MIN-uh-ruhlz):** Substances found in nature that are not plant or animal.

molecule **(MOL-uh-kyool):** A group of connected atoms.

pressure **(PRESH-ur):** The force of something pressing against something else.

saturated **(SACH-uh-ray-tuhd):** To be filled with something completely.

seed crystal **(SEED KRISS-tuhl):** A small crystal used to grow larger crystals.

supersaturation **(soo-pur-sach-ur-AY-shun):** The state of being filled beyond what there is room for.

For More Information

Books

Heather Moore Niver. *Crystals.* New York, NY: Rosen, 2017. This book gives readers an overview on crystals, including how they form.

Nancy Honovich. *Rocks & Minerals.* Washington, DC: National Geographic, 2016. This book helps readers identify different rocks and minerals and includes facts about the many types.

Serena Haines. *The Science of Gems.* Huntington Beach, CA: Teacher Created Materials, 2019. This book explores how minerals become gems and some of the different uses for gems.

Websites

DK Find Out: Crystals (https://www.dkfindout.com/us/earth/crystals-and-gems/crystals/) Students can learn about and explore photos of different kinds of crystals.

National Geographic Kids: Rocks and Minerals (https://kids.nationalgeographic.com/games/quizzes/quiz-whiz-rocks-minerals/) Students can test their knowledge of rocks and minerals and learn new facts about them.

Wonderopolis: Where Do Diamonds Come From? (https://www.wonderopolis.org/wonder/where-do-diamonds-come-from) This article teaches readers about the formation of diamonds.

Index

About the Author

Katie Chanez is a children's book writer and editor originally from Iowa. She enjoys writing fiction, playing with her cat, and petting friendly dogs. Katie now lives and works in Minnesota.